Transit

Transit

Cameron Awkward-Rich

Button Poetry / Exploding Pinecone Press
Minneapolis, Minnesota
2015

Published by Button Poetry / Exploding Pinecone Press
Minneapolis, MN 55403

http://buttonpoetry.com

Manufactured in the United States of America

Cover Design: Nikki Clark

ISBN 978-1-943735-01-3

CONTENTS

What's the use of being a boy if you are going to grow up to be a man?
—Gertrude Stein

...I felt as though I'd left myself behind. I didn't know what lay ahead but the train was hurtling through darkness toward that destination.
—Leslie Feinberg, *Stone Butch Blues*

ONCE

    you wanted to be beautiful
so rooted in your wet

dropped the seeds down
there & waited

to become a forest of sun-
flowers grown huge

as your mother
until you opened

your jaw & a tiny stone
spilled out

ESSAY ON THE THEORY OF MOTION

You remember reading a poem about a boy
driving his grandmother to the library across
town. Someone said that the car is a perfect
device for giving a poem the feeling of motion,
though you think the two must end up back at
the grandmother's house eventually, must walk
hallways lined with family ghosts, all smiling
through the window of a photograph & is that
motion, really? This tendency to cross & recross
the small terms of our own lives?

//

They expect me to talk about Newton. Fine. An
object at rest stays at rest. An object in motion
stays in motion. Friction has many names — it's
no surprise that when the train stops, so do you.

//

What else is true? You beg each thing to answer.
You make mouths for the answer to crawl
through. You bite the inside of your cheek. You
paint the world red all the way through.

//

I'm only kidding. You can't expect everything to
speak your language. To use these new mouths
for what you imagine mouths are for. After all,

4

you make a mouth on your upper thigh, the doctor calls it a wound, your dumb hands at work again. You can't get your body to tell the secret. Can't get it to tell you anything at all.

//

Anyway, you've begun to suspect that *theory* is less movement toward truth & more movement through a series of puns.

For example, a queer theorist—you don't know who, but imagine their white spectacled face floating above a soft butch sweater—once wrote that they feel most at home in airports, because there everyone is *in transition.*

//

(Let's get the obvious out of the way—you were a girl & then you weren't. You moved into a boy & the girl moved into misplaced language, into photographs.)

//

Get it? Gender is a country, a field of signifying roses you can walk through, or wear tucked behind your ear.

Eventually the flower wilts & you can pick another, or burn the field, or turn & run back across the tracks.

WHAT REMAINS

Up in the magnolia, the girl is a fleck of light
against more light. She doesn't block out the sun

filtering through velvet flowers
she doesn't brush away. Across the street

the boy with golden hair sings with the grass
between his fingers, while the girl next door laughs

& laughs, her mouth full of sweets. It's good
to know that life goes on like this in other children.

The girl has never had a mouth much good
for anything, but she's seen the whole block's

secrets—which grownups walk alone
at night, whose hand lingers on whose

shoulder blade. It's good, for now
there are things she doesn't understand—

what it means to go upstairs with a girl
whose skin is like her fading

flowers, what it means to be a thing
that doesn't keep the light out.

For now, there's a boy
making music. Not for her

but hers all the same.
She's filled by the sound

of other people. It's good
she can't understand

what this means yet. How easy
she can disappear.

BRIDGE

When she is a child
her father drives for hours

to sit with the bridge.
When she is still a child

full of hot tar, he tells her
she is the only reason he did not

jump. Her answer, pulled unflinching
from the city she carried there: *the river*

will so often open for another body, swallow it
so gently, but the pavement would have ruined you.

You tell this story over & over. It is easy.
As if it explains something, anything

about water or having once been
your father's girl. You will tell it again.

As if the telling will wear your cruelty
into grief, smooth & plain.

& what you leave out always
is when she is still a child—

the tar cooling & hardening
into an unfamiliar shape—

8

she dreams for years every sidewalk rising
to meet him like a swollen river.

What you leave out is the deep bruise
of the city as he splays & opens inside you.

It is only a dream—the nightmare is the version
in which his falling is perpetual. *When I am a child.*

When I am a child. Over & over. As if. The wet tar smell
the city carried, scraped & empty & you hate it—

your body. Or your father. Often
you cannot understand that difference.

THEORY OF MOTION (1)

When my sister drives me through the
winter at night, it is mostly in silence.
We believe in the economy of
language—you can say everything with
a few, plain words if someone is really
listening.

I spend this Christmas in the basement,
unwrapping letters from my high-
school love I've kept hidden in my
father's house. Strange

to think I ever was that person. A *me*
who didn't look up & see it coming. I
still don't know who was driving, or
what kind of animal we became.

When the car hits the deer my sister is
alone. Afterward, all she can say: *But the*
deer. I hit the deer. I killed her. She
watches us drive away & I want to
believe the doe stands

for something large, something other
than herself. But no matter how I freeze
her image in my mind, it is only a deer
& my sister is only a girl, ashamed &
sobbing in the backseat of her family's
car.

When we get home, dad throws around words like *insurance claim* & *photographic evidence* & stepmom wants to rehearse her story for the police. *What time was it? Why were you outside alone?*

& all I can do is stand over her like a house, like an older brother & worry about her leaving soon. Such a pretty girl, doe-eyed beneath her first boy's heaving engine. Her, shaking on the kitchen floor.

She isn't hurt, not really. No one blames her for the shattered night, the blood spilled across the sheet of snow come morning. *You couldn't see it coming,* I say. *You tried to stop. It wasn't your fault.*

The next day, the deer has vanished with the dark. All that matters now is the car, how to rehabilitate that wreckage. But there is still the image, still the animal wailing through our silence.

The deer. She cries. *I hit the deer. I killed her.*

THE INVISIBLE GIRL, 1996

This summer, all the coins beneath
the couch go missing, shoved

into her spotless palms.
Her father doesn't see her lift

bus tokens from his wallet, doesn't see
them float into her room like copper flies.

No one ever looks for her when things
disappear. After all, she is a little girl

& hardly there. The sun shines
through her chest as she rides

to the train across her town—glitter bike
piloting itself, streamers cutting the air

behind her & who in that white picket place
would have stopped her leaving? She makes it

all the way unseen, then drifts back
to her parents' doorway, such a lucky little girl

to be so unharmed, even they don't notice
she had gone.

ONCE

    you wanted to be a boy
so brought him

to your lips   drank
woke up not a boy

but never quite
yourself again

Essay on Waiting in Line

The other day I was at the post office. There was one person behind the desk—she hated her job & there was a line of twenty people, so we all hated her job too. In front of me this woman kept getting in & out of line until eventually she turned to me & said, *I just can't stand in this line. If I give you some money will you mail this package for me?* & I said *sure* & she handed me $3, told me to keep the change, smiling like she was the one doing me a favor.

The other day I was waiting in line at a hotel counter. I'd been there for ten minutes. I was the next person in line. Until two white ladies with suitcases the size of children rolled their bags right in front of me. I waited, I tried to give them the benefit of the doubt, but they rolled right up to the counter so I said *excuse me, I don't mean to be rude but...* & the air became a soundproof pane of glass I keep hitting up against.

The other day I was in the airport, waiting in line. Two white ladies in fur coats start pushing their way to the front, saying *excuse us, excuse us, we can't wait, we have a plane to catch!* Like the rest of us are just standing there for fun. Like we aren't all trying to get to the same place. Two minutes later, a woman & a red faced man walk the path the fur coats have cleared. The man is loud. The woman, terrified.

The other day, I was waiting in line at the reception for a person of color writing conference & then one white lady walks through the door, reaches through the line for the food on the table saying, *excuseme excuseme I know this is horribly rude...* but then another & another until there's a line of brown bodies with white hands reaching right through them.

The other day, forgive me, but I could have sworn I had a body. That it was solid & opaque & the story no one / everyone wants to hear is that the brown boy was no saint. That he got out of line. That he had to be put back in his place. But who could blame him, really? There has always been a woman with money. Or a fur coat. Or a mean husband.

Forgive me, white lady. I know, you know about waiting. You know about the step across the line & the red that sometimes follows. About hands reaching through you like you don't live in your skin, though you do, so you feel everything. I know you know about men with guns. With fists. With locked doors.

But the other day my professor (passes for a white lady) complains about getting a ticket for not waiting at a red light

& the other day a cop (white lady) scolds my
mother like a naughty child

& the other day a boy is killed & no one can
wash his blood from their tongues

& the other day a trans woman is killed & her
body does not make a sound

& in the beginning, a slave girl is raped by her
master & his wife (white lady) orders the skin
torn from her back for the crime of having a
body at all

I know, I know, we're all just trying to get to
the same place

& so the other day, forgive me, but how could I
care if the boy had also had a gun?

THIN

Small emergencies this morning—
none of the pants fit & you have to be

in public. As the train pulls you underwater
you try to remember the last time

you touched someone else on purpose
& today closes & opens again as a room

where your body does not exist.
What is it that breaks your heart

exactly? Makes you a coastline
losing yourself in increments?

It's still morning here for other people
but you remember so clearly facing yourself

in the mirror. That wasn't yesterday?
You aren't a girl with fistfuls

of skin & a mouth like a house fire?
You won't swallow everything, then beg

for more?   You guess the train
is where you go now to feel back at home.

To feel like time isn't something that just happens
to you—open your eyes & there goes a day, a week,

a country, a name. On the train, nothing's left behind
but miles. You don't lose anything you haven't paid to

& anyway most days you know you'll get them back.
You know you'll sit inside the moving hallway

of your loneliness & won't pry
open any doors. Here, everyone can see you.

Everyone would watch you vanish & the magic
would be lost. Your whole life whittled down

to fiction. You know, the one about a boy who fell
in love with his own image. Who tried to make himself

a bridge. Who wanted so badly to kiss the dark
that he became it.

What's Lost

The girl

in the story

kisses the boy

behind the school

house & then

there she is laid

beneath the honey

suckle training

her tongue

to coax the nectar

to her mouth

in this story

she has a mouth

THEORY OF MOTION (2): THE SEX QUESTION

The only words I have to explain it
are not the kind anyone wants to hear—

You look just like a headless chicken, darling
or *I love the way you are so like a puppet*

made of meat. How I can slip my hand inside
& make you sing sweet & just for me.

Ok, maybe the headless chicken thing
needs further explanation—

Tonight, I want you to pluck the bird
from my throat. To be the dumb singing

animal. I want to watch you change
behind your eyes & pull feathers

from your teeth. See, I do want
to learn to leave

without blood. So maybe *headless chicken*
is the wrong image after all. Maybe

it's more like *woodpecker in a room*
made of glass. Maybe my question is—

what does it feel like to be thrown wide
open? & where do you go once I've shattered

all the windows, once there's nothing left
to beat your wings against but the drenched air

outside? Tonight, I want you to train me
to fly. That's better, right? To call it *flight*

& not *the meat's idiot dance once the boy
has left the building?* Me, I've wanted

to be a thousand things. I've got names
for all of them & as many kinds

of travel—the knife, the needle, the wolf
in bird's clothes. I say *take me* & I mean

*darling, teach me to dance from the wet ruins
of myself.* I mean *I have a question, an image*

a feathered head in my mouth.

THE INVISIBLE GIRL, 2014

We plunge into the dark beneath the bay
& then I become it—

Yo homie, I bet you think you're cute, bet you got mad
bitches begging to suck your dick.

He goes on like this from SF to Oakland.
The man, pale & harmless in his business

suit, grips the back of an invisible girl's neck
as she works his cock right there on the train.

Don't you think I know this story?
Black boy hung, black boy bruised

fruit on the vine, black boy torn
open for having seeds at all

I used to stand in the kitchen with the women.
We peeled the potatoes. Sometimes we cut our hands

& cooked the blood right in. I learned to be a good girl
didn't I? To bleed & then set the table. Call the boys in

to feast. A wound that never heals. That's what they call it,
right? We all know what they mean.

Sometimes I fear the first man's seed bloomed into a boy
who grew & grew into the one who wears my body.

That the girl's turned blue, floated to the surface
& then out my skin—

& it's strange, you know, to be split. To be two things
at once. The fruit & the knife at once. Hunger & the feast.

That night I got off the train. I looked
in the mirror. I found his face.

ONCE

you wanted to be dead
outside your window

the grass was dead
& because you couldn't move

through glass or move at all
you laid in bed for years

mouthing   *lawnmower*
  lawnmower

Essay on Crying in Public

In the movie theatre, I hold my mother's lean wrist in my bird-boned hand while she weeps right through the closing scene of *Despicable Me 2*.

The protagonist, an ex-supervillain, finally leans in to kiss the girl & it's almost like my mother is a woman who cries at endings, but I remember sitting like this at her mother's funeral, how her eyes were dull stones slouching in her face.

//

My mother believes most problems can be solved with statistics. I conduct an experiment:

I turn off all the lights.

I say   *love is a journey.*
I say   *love is a house.*
I say   *love is a fire.*
I say   *love is a burning house cast out in the night.*

I believe clichés should reveal the truth about things, since truth is only what we call it & this is how statistics work.

//

I discover that my mother can't remember how she met my father.

The story, as she tells it: she went abroad, got malaria & when she returned my father bought her a bottle of wine, wasn't interested in dating & then they had been married for ten years & he was leaving.

Memory, too, is a problem of language. To call you my friend? My wife? My love, my editor, my pet? I don't know. Already you move hazy through my life & then out of it again.

//

My housemate says that public transit crying is the worst—then you know sadness will rear its wild head, despite the prescription bridle, the years of mastering the body. I think of you. The train wails against the tracks & I mistake that sound for my own.

//

I conduct an experiment:

I attempt to cry the distance between my house & my work. Two whole hours of tears. Enough to make the woman next to me shake her head, embarrassed for both of us. Not enough to drown her, or choke on my own silt.

Most people just stare through me like I am, in fact, the sulfurous water outside their windows. One woman, mistaking me for someone who could be her grandson, holds out a handful of hard candy, asks me why I'm so sad.

I'm not, I tell her, *I'm conducting an experiment. About what?* she asks. *Love, my mother's stubborn optimism, the possibility of exhausting grief in anticipation of great loss. Oh,* she says. *Yes, precisely.*

THEORY OF MOTION (3): MDMA

        & I sit at the bar all night
alone & almost don't hate the world of
limbs writhing beneath the strobe
lights. *Incredible.* How you can rinse the
brain with chemical joy & still this
wicked film coats everything behind
the eyes.

My housemate, swaying in the static
air, asks if I *like the music,* if it *feels good*
& because I cannot translate this into
any language that I recognize, I smile.
I show her all my teeth.

The music throbs like a fist through
drywall & it does *feel good* & the
specters shine beneath it & I want to
want to reach out, to touch, to name
the widening gap between desire & my
fevered lust for quiet, forever quiet.

Across the dance floor, the rest of me
stands pinned to a boy, precisely
because he will never turn to look at
me & if he did would not see my
hunger in this shape. *Incredible.* How
you can pay a man to slice away the
softest parts of you. Leave her behind
in the metal of the surgery but, always,

you are that red, red child huddled in
the corner, clutching her mother's one
good kitchen knife.

Theory of Motion (4): Another Middle-Class Black Kid Tries to Name It

I used to dream about a woman trapped inside
a burning house. That isn't how she went—

my grandmother. Instead, her city moved
inside her like a drunk man's fist.

All I know about my father's mother are these holes
in her, the holes she left. My father, pulled over

to the side of the road, crying a song
through the radio. I think her grief moved

into my father when he was born & into his daughters
when we were born & I'm sure someone's tried

to tell you the blues is only music, *but the radio
the radio.*

                          //

Once, my teacher bought me a cheeseburger & asked
how come the other black kids weren't more like me.

Once, a girl pinned me to the wall until I called myself
(or her) *nigga* & all week I wore her fingers as a bruise.

Once, I watched my teacher tell that other brown girl
her language was too beautiful to belong to her.

Those years, I wore cargo shorts through the winter,
books in each pocket, little hallways full of words
that weren't our own.

                         //

Is there a word for a child talking to himself
or no one?   I've said *ghost*

but I do have skin & a father, after all. Hands
after all, dirt colored & not buried in the dirt.

Sure, I've been opened the way girls are opened.
Sure, I've gone missing in the dark.

Sure, I've looked at my sister & seen a woman
caught in flames. But we have pills for that.

We have money for pills for that.

                         //

Please—

what's the word for being born of sorrow
that isn't yours? For having a family?

For belonging nowhere? Not even
your body. Especially not there.

THE CHILD FORMERLY KNOWN AS ____

is what your father calls you now.   Yes, you know
your father loves you
            but each time he will not name you

                  you feel a hole
bang open.   Black pit.   Runs straight through you
      like a tunnel,
                  which is what it is.

There are tracks laid in the tunnel in you & a train.
                              Yes, that's right, a train
            & on the other end, a little girl.

      The train is where each thing made for her
                              that happens in your life
goes to travel to her & sometimes
                  you think you will die—

last night the man tugging at his crotch
            says *Have a good night girl* or maybe he doesn't
            grab his crotch & means nothing or means well
      but what does it matter?
                        He boards the train
with your father & your first girlfriend & the state of Michigan
                  & they all want to see the girl

& you're carrying a train full of people who want you gone
                        or think you are gone.

But then the train is full & leaves
                     its station & leaves the hole
                                 engine warm & then
     it all feels   faintly ridiculous—

who does that man think you are, anyway?
Even if you are a girl, you don't look like the kind who would
                                  want him, though you do
      in another life where he says *girl*
        with a slightly different inflection
& means he is the kind of man who wants a boy to ruin him.
                  To carve a hole & move inside.

         But that isn't how it happened.
         You're the one with the hole

with the little girl inside the hole
      with the father standing at the edge, calling & calling
         for her & never you
            & you can't blame him—

     you'd rather be her
         or at least bury her, seal her shut
or shut her up
           & in the end, isn't that what we all want?

        To not feel so
split?   To carry an image of ourselves
        inside ourselves & know exactly what we mean

    when we say *I*—   .   *I*—   .

     I—?

ONCE

    you ate a field of snow
with a teaspoon & forgot

language altogether, couldn't stand
the thought of moving

through so many
spoiled mouths.

Theory of Motion (5)

The April I knew we would not outlast winter, we drove down the coast to swelter in a rented room. We drove to Virginia, then kept driving out into the ocean to an island we'd both read about as kids.

In the stories, there was a shipwreck hundreds of years ago—no one survived but the horses that fought their way to shore, coats all gone matted.

They say that once a wild horse learns to eat from a person's palm, once her fear has been trained back out, she will hand herself over to the slaughter. After all, what's the difference between a hand concealing something sweet & a hand moving behind the window of a car? & you, before we walked out to where the horses grazed, you bought two apples—Pink Ladies. Quartered them with the knife your father gave you before your hands were strong enough to hold it.

I don't know if that part's true, or if I care. I wasn't listening, I admit. I was watching a bird thrash the glass surface of a lake, like it was trying to break back into the dark.

I forgot about that island until years later, riding home alone underneath the bay, then breaking through to a fevered sky. Something panicked in my chest & I cried for hours, missed my stop on purpose, lunatic grinning from between my wet fingers.

Winter is the season of wanting everyone to look at me. To watch me stand & shake the flies from my back, to watch me leave without language or reason. Each year, I think I have finally outgrown youth's obligatory madness. Swear to never fall in love again with a hand that always gives me what I ask for.

But there's someone on fire in the attic & no one knows how she got there or where she came from. Though it's simple really. See how we've left it so far behind us? *The horses? The lake? The apples? The bird?* Most of the time that's all there is—we leave, eat a nice dinner, go back to our hotel room & fuck. Simple.

Until it breaks & suddenly you've killed an entire island of horses. Suddenly childhood slams shut & it's all your fault. I was sprawled in your kitchen, the animals moving through the blood in my hands. I held them out to you like fruit. I think they were beautiful. I think I was glad we'd driven to Virginia & fought the whole way. I think I owe you an apology, I think I must have loved you, I keep rewriting this story—who are you? A bird? Or a boy? Or an image of a boy with frantic wings, trying to outrun my changing weather?

WHAT RETURNS

So now winter is a place I visit
but don't belong to. I pass the time

in a room that isn't childhood, but
does that matter? My mother

is still down the hall & I am still
watching men on screen break

into other men & the once-snowfield
of my body becomes a flood that shatters

me each night. I thought I was finished
with desire & what a relief. To not want

to reach outside the skin. To touch
what isn't mine, or anything at all.

To not be a tongue in a glass jar
in an ocean. But the pills make me

dream in oceans. I wake up crusted
with someone else's salt.

I become a boy who touches
the backs of strangers' necks

in public—in love with the soft
of his own throat.

This makes every man
on the train into something

that could kill me. Don't worry.
That's a good thing.

It means I got on the train.
It means I still have a body.

THEORY OF MOTION (6), NOCTURNE

for them all

I try not to write about these ghosts.
As if this too does not turn a child

to narrative. As if this too does not demand
a kind of work. But boy after boy after boy

after boy after girl after sweet outline of a boy—
& have you ever known a body not to be haunted?

Ever known a black body not to be riddled
with light?

                    //

We buried my great-grandmother in 2008.
She was 95. She survived so much.

If I have to tell you what I mean
then she's not yours to carry.

If I have to tell you, well, here's a gate
opening in the poem. Here's an exit.

Walk through.

                    //

My great-grandmother was named Violet.
Violet. She had six sisters, a garden

of black girls. Imagine naming your girl-
child for a flower. Imagine doing this

over & over again. Imagine a flower, how easy
to ruin for want of a little color

to decorate the kitchen. Imagine tearing up
handfuls of blossoms. Imagine pressing them

into a girl's dim shape, to say, *This is you.*
This is what the world has made of you.

Now imagine she lived
& she lived.

                    //

Once, I was a girl
who took a black boy's name

into her mouth. I don't know a thing
about bullets, but I sure do know

about holes.

ONCE

I admit you may have gone
too far, wanting

words to mean what they mean
but who can blame you?

    you were given a name.

(Vagina Monologue)

It would be so easy to think the boy hardened over the wound of me but that isn't true. Just because I was stone once & everything a child with a hammer standing over me & just because we know how that story goes doesn't mean I won't say the words. Doesn't mean I won't sing. & another thing—the boy is a boy & there are countless ways to wreck what must be wrecked, but aren't I the river he will lead the man to drink & then be drowned? Here, the world vanishes inside him & never again the other way around.

ACKNOWLEDGMENTS

The first draft of this chapbook was written mostly in the summer of 2014, while I was "co-coaching" the first & only New Sh!t Show National Poetry Slam team. Without that summer of workshop & brunch, *Transit* would not exist. So, thank you to: Sam Sax, Nic Alea, Danez Smith, Jason Bayani, Tatyana Brown, Joshua Merchant, & Jelal Huyler.

Some of these poems, sometimes under different names & in different shapes, have appeared in the following publications: *The Seattle Review, Revolution House, Hobart, Tandem, The Bakery, & Nepantla*. Many thanks to these editors for believing in my work.

Finally, thanks to Button Poetry for giving this little book a home & good company.

About the Author

Cameron Awkward-Rich is the author of *Sympathetic Little Monster* (Ricochet Editions, 2016). A Cave Canem fellow and Poetry Editor for *Muzzle Magazine*, his poems have appeared/are forthcoming in *The Journal, The Offing, Vinyl, cream city review* and elsewhere. Cam is currently a doctoral candidate in Modern Thought & Literature at Stanford University. Find him at cawkwardrich.com.